SCHIRMER'S LIBRARY OF MUSICAL CLASSICS

J. B. DUVERNOY

Op. 120

THE SCHOOL OF MECHANISM

Fifteen Studies for the Piano

WRITTEN EXPRESSLY TO PRECEDE
CZERNY'S SCHOOL OF VELOCITY

Edited and Fingered
by
KARL KLAUSER

ISBN 978-0-7935-5935-0

G. SCHIRMER, *Inc.*

DISTRIBUTED BY

 HAL•LEONARD®
CORPORATION
7777 W. BLUEMOUND RD. P.O. BOX 13819 MILWAUKEE, WI 53213

School of Mechanism.

J. B. DUVERNOY. Op. 120.

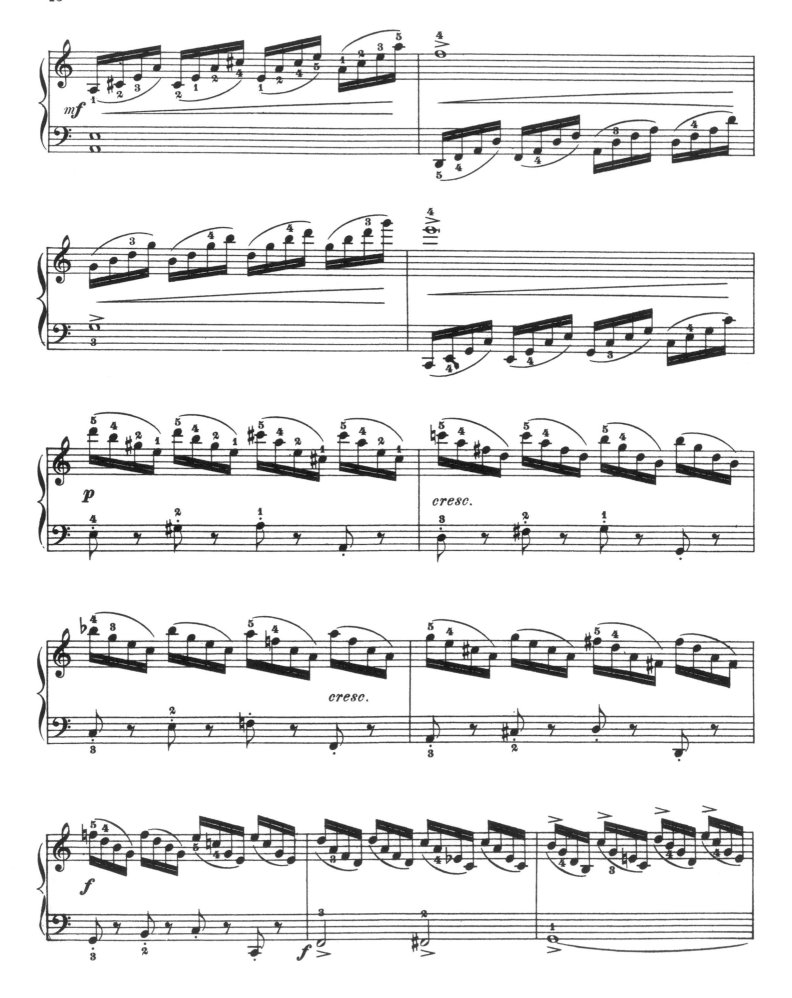

Fine.

cresc. poco a poco.

cresc. poco a poco.

D. S.

14

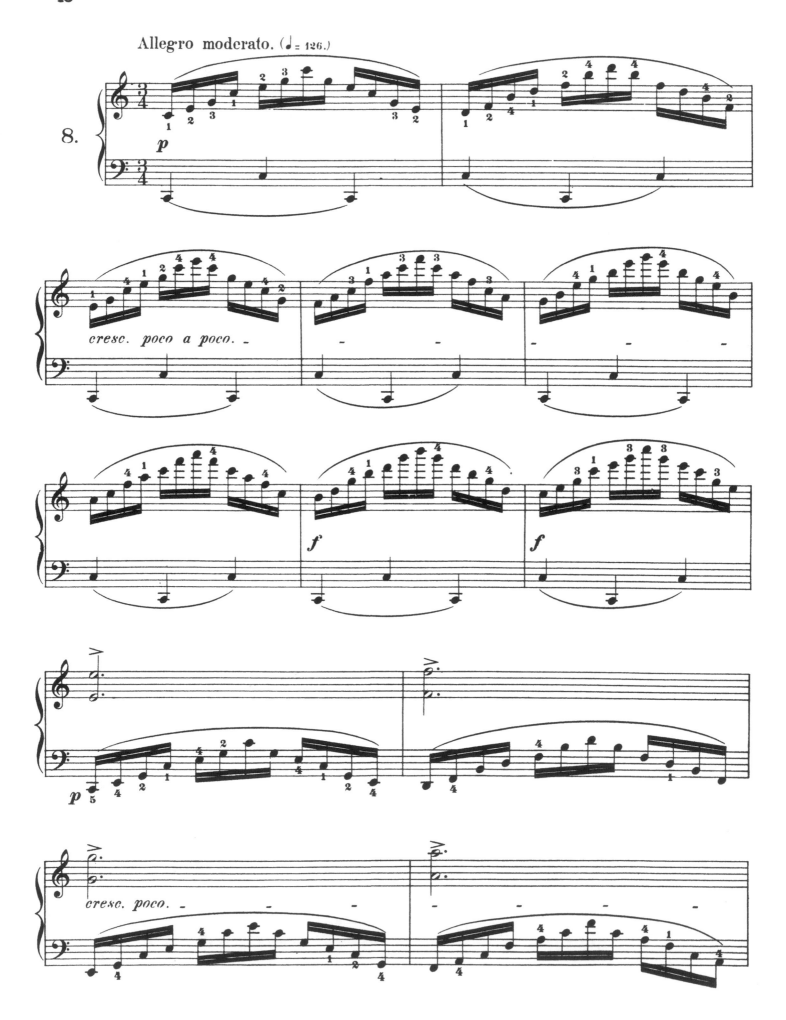

Allegro moderato. (♩ = 126.)

9.

10.

11.

12.

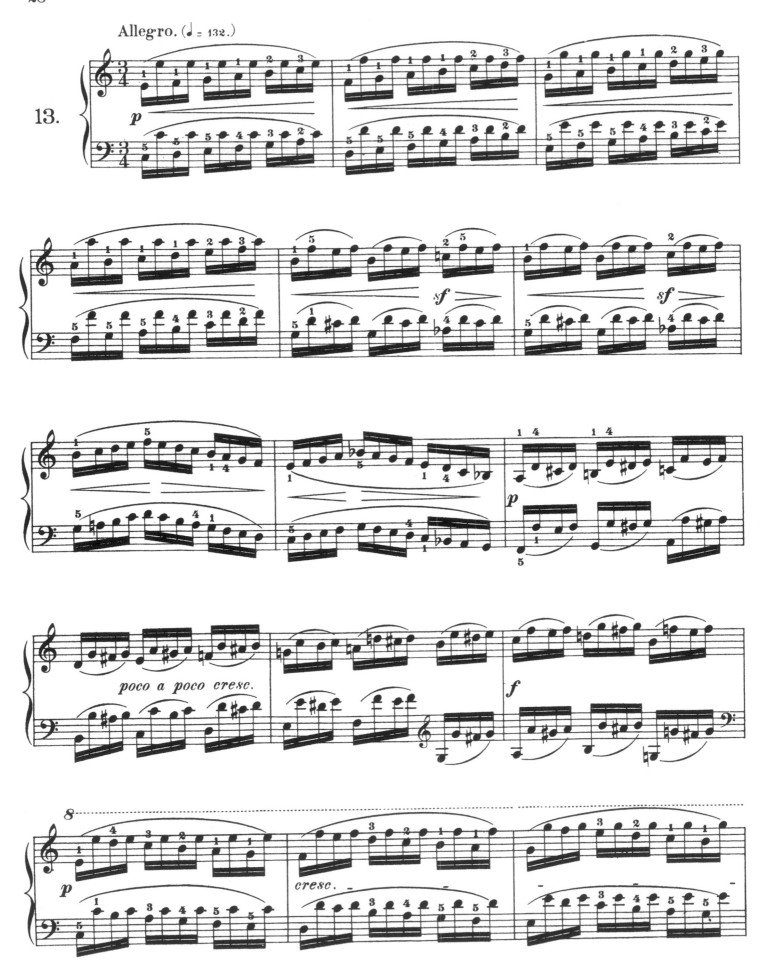

Moderato. (♩ = 120.)
il canto espressivo.

15.

ben sostenuto.

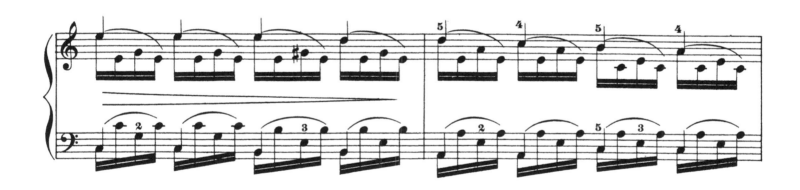

dim.

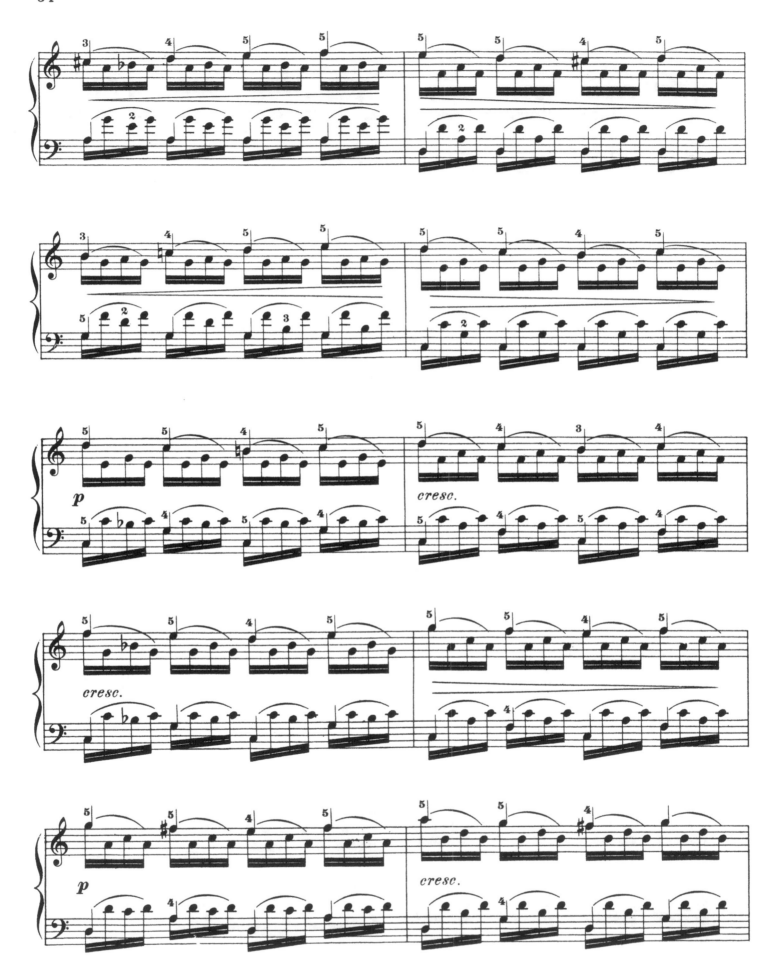

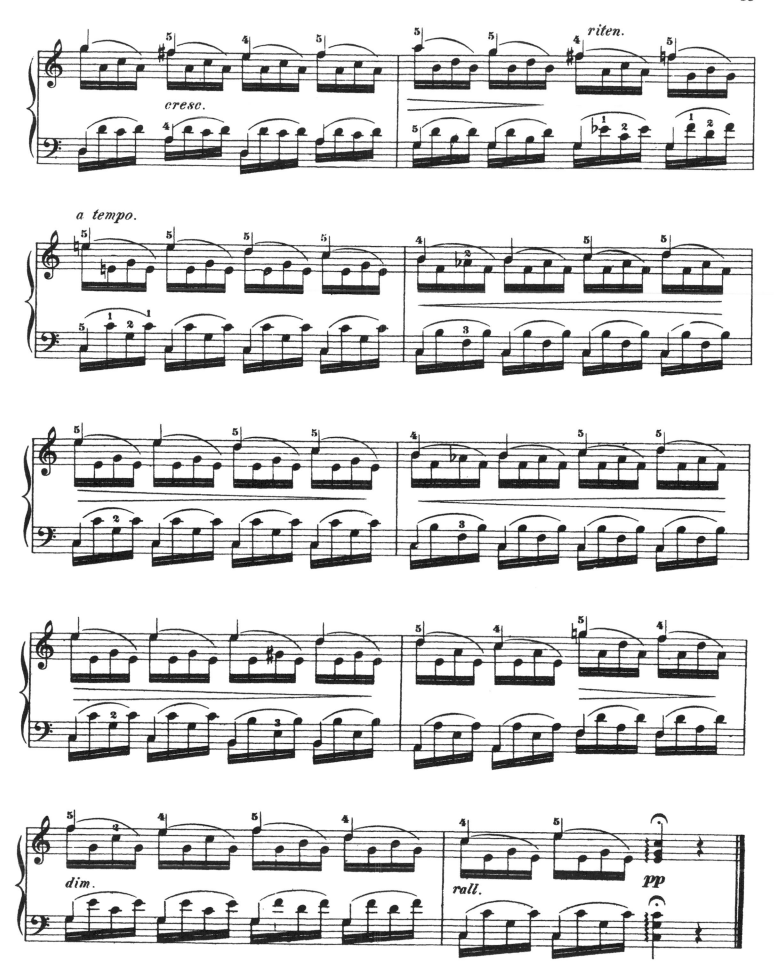